Ramblings Through Time
2020 – A Year to Remember

Times That Try the Soul

MK Brennan

Dedicated with admiration to those who brought grace, care, dignity, love, and support to individuals around the world during the COVID-19 pandemic, especially the healthcare providers and researchers.

Also dedicated with sympathy to those who suffered loss and grief.

Last, but certainly not least, this is dedicated with gratitude to all who participated in the Saturday Songwrite (SSW) sessions that started on March 21, 2020 with Gary Lightbody. The global community that came together through those sessions has been a true blessing during an isolating period of time for so many around the world, sparking friendships and creativity.

Introduction

The year 2020 will be memorialized for decades to come, perhaps centuries. It started fairly calm in most parts of the world. Incubating and spreading, however, was a new coronavirus in Wuhan, China. It found its way to Europe, Australia, North America, South America, Africa, and other parts of Asia. A global pandemic changed all expectations for the year. Isolation and lockdown, masks and social distancing became the norms. All businesses were impacted, causing unemployment, food insecurity, a decrease in supplies, and so much more. So many questions about the virus itself and the best treatments. So many needs for those infected. So little equipment for the hospitals and the healthcare providers. Scrambling for answers in what seemed like a split second.
In the United States, the too age-old problem of racial disparity was also triggered by the ongoing killing of persons of color at the hands of police officers. Protests calling for justice spread around the world. Rioting occurred that blurred the line of the message for some.

Then there was the US Presidential election that took directions one could never expect to happen in the modern world. Events related to it took a tragic turn on January 6, 2021 with the storming of the Capitol building resulting in the death of 5 individuals. My intent when putting thoughts for this book together was taking it through to the inauguration on January 20, 2021 thinking that would be a good endpoint. The writings included here extend a bit beyond that date.

The words shared on the following pages were written throughout the year, starting in May, which is when I decided to start putting pen to paper in earnest. There is one piece that was written in March about the refugees who waited to come into our country. My heart has belonged to those who strive to seek a better life for themselves and their families for many decades so starting this book with thoughts of them seems appropriate to me. Proceeds from the sale of this book will be donated to Annunciation House, https://annunciationhouse.org/, "a volunteer organization that offers hospitality to migrants, immigrants, and refugees in the border region of El Paso, Texas."

My hope is that a word or two shared here will touch you or spark some thoughts that you have about the topics.

"Words are like nets – we hope they'll cover what we mean, but we know they can't possibly hold that much joy, or grief, or wonder." Author Jodi Picoult, *Change of Heart*

TABLE OF CONTENTS

March 2020

As the month unfolded, attention moved to a new coronavirus that first came to light in some parts of the world in January and February. In the United States, those months focused on the impeachment hearings of the President and the emerging narrowing of the field of Democratic candidates for the Presidential election to be held in November. I had been writing some poems here and there but nothing in earnest over these months and not ones that spoke to national or global events. However, refugees have always been held close in my heart and the ongoing lack of compassion by the administration in power pained me. The one poem for this month speaks to that and it also was the second time that I put the words to music as I started guitar lessons during this time.

Distant Voices

The misty haze of the morning
Greets me at the water's edge
Memories of a touch, a connection
Now fall silent in the aching of my heart

Gone to empty chairs and distant voices
Unheard but loudly shouting out
In the silence listen to their pleadings
They're the salt of the earth who long for hope

A gift to one another
Dusty roads and winding hills
Golden sunsets, huddled masses
Calling out in the darkness to us all

Gone to empty chairs and distant voices
Unheard but loudly shouting out
In the silence listen to their pleadings
They're the salt of the earth who long for hope

They're the salt of the earth who long for hope

March 28, 2020 mkb

May 2020

So much news in April and May set the course for the summer ahead. Lockdowns around the world, ongoing denials of the severity of COVID-19 in the US with calls by many to re-open, ongoing election campaigning, and on Memorial Day, the killing of George Floyd at the knee of a police officer. Polarization and divisiveness that had been ongoing took on expanded levels. Throughout all of it, there were also many examples of care and some unity around the world as efforts were joined to address the pandemic and help support healthcare providers and those who lost jobs, faced food shortages, and suffered from the illness or the death of a loved one.

Copperheads to Cardinals

From copperheads to cardinals
There's a knowing of the earth
A divine presence in measured tension
All in timing as we plot our course

The phoenix rises from ashes
A lesson to be learned
Take all that has been provided now
Rebuild a path on firmer ground

These are the rules or so was said
Once thought as truths but now are dead
Only one boat in the storm
Only one person to love
Only one race of humans
Only one God to revere
Only one melody to sing

You flipped me sideways in my thinking
New adventures to have
My heart now able to embrace
What up 'til now, could not be faced

You speak your mind so clearly
Integrity in your soul
The way that once was lost is clear
Everything falling in place now dear

These are the rules or so was said
Once thought as truths but now are dead
Only one boat in the storm
Only one person to love
Only one race of humans
Only one God to revere
Only one melody to sing

May 19, 2020 mkb with a nod to John O'Donohue and Gary Lightbody for concepts or a few words used here

Inspiring Collaboration

How do we inspire love, peace, hope
In the face of all the hatred and pain
I look in your eyes and only see your care
Your heart and soul are gentle
And determined, wanting to right wrongs
To understand how any of this could be

How do we start to live well together
When it just feels that we're falling back
Away from all that is full of grace
We are teetering on the edge
On the brink of a world undefined
Where is the path to be taken now

How do we break through the clouds
That darken the skies with despair and dread
Where is the hope amidst the fear
There's just a blur of grey covering the day
Light one more candle and then another
Make a gentle noise like sighs on a summer breeze

How do we keep our hearts alive and caring
When it feels like we're holding goodbye in our hands
Call out to one another to show the way
We're not finished – we have just begun
Helping each other to feel not so lost and alone
Lighting one candle and another through actions and words

mkb 5/31/2020; inspired by SSW 5/30/2020, the protests following George Floyd's
murder, and the SpaceX launch

June 2020

Many parts of the world came together for a new reason this month as peaceful protests were held in more than 60 countries following the death of George Floyd. Black Lives Matter was echoed far and wide but not by all. More conflicts ensued as US leadership took a hardline against peaceful protesters, including a time tear gas was used against them all for a publicity pose. COVID continued to spread in parts of the US while there were some indications that it was beginning to slow in others. With the ongoing election campaigns, divisiveness continued to impact communities.

Sides

There's a certain numbness
That settles in the heart
Outrage often turns to complacency
As yet another senseless act occurs

Truth – Lies
Right – Wrong
Up – Down
Over – Out
What is real
Some divide and will wither
Others join and will grow

Thoughts and prayers are buzzwords
While melancholy and anger battle to be heard
Whose side are you on with this one
There are always sides to be taken

Two sides to a coin but that's not all
Eight sides to a stop sign but when will it stop
Polygons, multisided, multidimensional
Multifaceted kaleidoscope of light and dark

Truth – Lies
Right – Wrong
Up – Down
Over – Out
What is real
Some divide and will wither
Others join and will grow

Missing something I barely knew
Missing something I thought I knew
Heaviness surrounds the days
Absorb, revolt, absolve, resolve

June 4, 2020 mkb

Paradox

Where to start
So many thoughts
Hard to focus
Clear vision dimmed
Feeling the way back
From a time long ago but new
Routine upended days before
Not important in the light of day
Or dark of night
Fears uncovered, anger rising
Peel back layers of hope and love
Find the core of understanding
Carry On and... what, how, why
What can be taught
What can be learned
What does the climate allow
What does the climate provide
In a world of double speak
Divergent ideologies
Altered perceptions and perspectives
Explore the possibilities
Move beyond privileged fantasies
See the phoenix rise in the sky
Light the candle in day and night
One moment, one decision
Can make or break
Search the hearts
Search the souls
Search the minds
Discover
Time hurts, time heals
Once truth prevails
Where is truth

mkb 6/8/2020
(paradox: a situation that combines contradictory features or qualities)

Garden of Eden

Families grieve
Loss of loved ones
Countries mourn
Loss of humanity
It's time to march

Global voices rise and move
From clapping in doorways
Singing from balconies
Bells ringing for carers
To righteous indignation

A hundred million puzzle pieces
Are spread on the table
Persons with hierarchy of needs
Turn this chaos to clarity
Lead by example

Platitudes met with action
Not staged prop shows
Love thy neighbor negated
Then reinforced
 Waves of reactions, responses

So many changes
So little time
What will remain
Who will decide
What no longer serves

All under one sky
Sun rises, sun sets
Moon phases guide the sea
Seasons come and go
Natural flow of life

We have all that is needed
Garden of Eden provided
Who still bites the poison
Who will still be the snake
As families grieve and countries
mourn

June 8, 2020 mkb

Now What Normal

Hello normal
Just calling out
There's talk of a new you
Is that true
Or more of SSDD
With steps forward
Then leaps back
A world in jumbles
Shut down, lock down
Open here, reclose there
Death counts daily
One in the street
That leaves us reeling
March on, march on
Feel the discomfort
Explore the pain
Mourn it all
Find a way back
To a place now changed
With hope as life rafts
In a sea of turbulent waters

Negotiate, legislate, regulate
Rebuild hearts and spirits
Open eyes and minds
Yard signs, painted roads
Superficial or more
Catalyst for change
See differences
Seek
Repeat history or rewrite
New day on horizon
What will emerge
Hello normal
Just calling out
Where are you
What are you these days
There's talk of a new you
Is that true
Or more of SSDD

June 12, 2020 mkb

Painting Hope

Signs of hope
Rising – Fleeting
From one day to another
As knot in stomach loosens
Pain in heart increases
Open wound covered
Festering below layers of gauze
Unpack it and try to cleanse
Course of treatment debated
Seek healing of hearts
Of minds, of spirits
Paint a new day picture
Not with false promises
Or false premises
Draw from history
Draw from love
Draw from peace
Draw from respect
Draw from kindness
Draw from liberty
And justice for ALL
Show up, show your receipt
Reach out – educate
Listen – Listen – Listen

June 15, 2020 mkb

Not Moving – Ode to COVID

Calling out the last thing on my mind
Was it a million years ago or just yesterday
Time is relative or so I've heard
Who are these relations that they say

When we started out on this journey
Everything was grand and felt like a mini vacay
Noon tea with Mary, her dog, and cat
Songs with Gary, Steve, Mark, Vin, and Jay

Projects new and old started and done
Ear savers for healthcare workers among the lot
All this filled the time quite nicely
With new friends writing from all about

More than three months now, the grand is gone
Projects half done, peace lily neglected and dead
Calendar on the wall marked COVID
Month after month with a sense of dread

Song dates have waned, fatigue setting in
Organizing drawers and shelves long lost their appeal
YouTube, Netflix, Amazon all on
Moving from couch, the struggle is real

It will get better or so I hope
They tell me we're just waiting for the last to go
So be gentle with yourself for now
Soon enough we all will know?

June 24, 2020 mkb

July 2020

Events from previous months took on heightened awareness. Heated debates about public health initiatives to help stem the spread of COVID were being played out across the US and at the highest levels of government. For the November election, one campaign side encouraged the use of the initiatives in light of the pandemic. The other side started to put doubt about the safety and validity of any votes done in this way. Soon thereafter, post office slowness was noticed. As ongoing debate and discussion was held about the peaceful protests and Black Lives Matter. A civil rights icon, John Lewis, died from cancer, and former President Obama spoke eloquently at his funeral. The month continued the divisiveness that seemed to be the brush painting each and every topic and event.

Look in the Mirror

Sitting with uncomfortable thoughts
Challenged to look long and hard
In the mirror of bias
Honestly let down my guard

Face up to some facts long held
Based on stories told through years
Need to check ego at door
Explore buried views and fears

Underneath the surfaces
Images held in my brain
Trying to get through the door
To understand all the pain

Open mind, accepting all
Had been an honest belief
Recent days call to reflect
As nations unite in grief

In faith have been accepting
Of many races and creeds
Others choices for their love
Over the years in words and deeds

Truth be told I dare reveal
Have held back understanding
Those not similar to me
In interests and standing

Grew up with mixed messages
Love each other as thy own
But some fall below that bar
Through no fault of theirs alone

Place of birth is not chosen
Yet determines much in life
Education and a home
Live with privilege or with strife

We tend to hang with our own
There's a language and a norm
Experiences we share
Common lives in shape and form

Those outside our little spheres
Are often misunderstood
Stereotypes are created
Often set in stone for good

Repeated time and again
I hold some of those it seems
Held down in the recesses
Hidden deeper than my dreams

Inner city strikes a chord
Left over from years gone by
Troubles in another land
Kept me away I cannot lie

Breaking down those stony walls
Is not that easy to do
Facing that some thoughts are held
Is a way to start anew

Get to know those from places
Not familiar in my days
Can bring a change to the view
Set a path for newer ways

Examine those thoughts from past
Look for lies now unfounded
Filter through ideas that creep
And check for truths now grounded
July 1, 2020 mkb

Who's to Blame

A man was killed on the street
A woman in her bed
Another in his car
And one while jogging up ahead

Within months of each other
Truly a lifetime for them
Who's to blame for their loss
How do we write their requiem

Easy to point to the one on his knee
The one with the gun in hand
What of the more global blame
The one that society commands

So many names on the wall
So many more than those above
Over the decades, over the years
Taken too soon from those they love

Labels and names of degradation
Called out to those oppressed
Passed down through generations
Too often that are put to the test

Questions raised but not answered
To the satisfaction of those in need
Rules and regulations set in place
That hinder any progress indeed

Cain killed Abel so it's said
Is that where all this hatred started
Will there ever be an end to see
When we don't grieve the murdered departed

In the immediate, we take to the streets
We call for justice to be served
Donations are made here and there
With all of that, will those calling out be heard

Who knows how to best fix this mess
Will it ever truly mend
In reality, person to person sharing
May help many of us comprehend

We can legislate and regulate
Talk until blue in the face
But until we walk in other's shoes
Not sure we can be one human race

July 2, 2020 mkb

The Jack in the Box

The jack in the box
Has sprung its spring
Flailing about
A wayward "king"

The court healer
Has tried so hard
Authoring edicts
Sending the guard

The jester laughs
In the far corner
Cowering alone
Hiding the mourner

Percy arrives
With mask intact
Keeps a safe distance
Avoids close contact

He stands alone
Others ignore
The best of advice
And head out the door

Parties are lively
Drinks and a dance
Sunning and swimming
All taking a chance

Numbers are climbing
Young ones at risk
Beds at a premium
The fire is brisk

Rain clouds are needed
To send a downpour
And cover the land
Give them what for

July 6, 2020 mkb

Distant Connection

How do I tell you
What's to be said
So much has happened
Jumbled thoughts in my head

Adjustments and changes
Are needed these days
Explore new adventures
Find other ways

Weeks apart have been trying
Too much time on my own
My life is redundant
Confined to my home

You grace my screen daily
In old times we shared
Saved as a video
That shows how you cared

Today you return
With a smile on your face
There is a peace and an ease
Comfort all over the place

Still at a distance
The connections remain
I touch the screen gently
As you call out my name

It is here that we'll be
For some more time it seems
Restrictions do hold us
But can't limit our dreams

July 8, 2020 mkb

Real World Creeps

Holes in the fabric
Flaws in the system
Underlying causes
Unraveling the hem

Seams at the bursting
Balloons pop in air
Fiction, non-fiction
How do they compare

What is real
What is fake
Who to trust
Who to forsake

Outside force coming in
Reveals all the smoke
And mirrors held high
To all that is broke

Systemic infection
Down to the core
Greed and corruption
But wait there is more

Suppression, oppression
Of that group or this
Over the decades
Through the abyss

What is real
What is fake
Who to trust
Who to forsake

Few are the chosen
Who don't pay the price
Yet hold all the power
And roll the high dice

Real world now creeps
Shows all of the flaws
Who will step up now
To rewrite the laws

July 8, 2020 mkb

Which Way is Up

It's hard not to get complacent
It's easy to just let go
Forget all of the differences
Try to just move with the flow
But conscious has its reasons
To ever pull one back
Try to go and make a difference
For all those things that lack
Like respect for one another
And hearts that can be true
To ease the pain of others
To try something anew
How can we be together
When forces pull apart
Things that are outside the walls
Yet dictate lives from the start
We question and strive to seek
Answers to what's what
All have different stories
Hard to know which way is up

July 8, 2020 mkb

Passing Blame

It's not mine
It was the dog
It was the weather
It was the day of the week
It was the hour of the day

What excuses do we make
For mistakes that are made
Or things we should have done
Passing the blame
The new/old game

The world is held captive
At this time or that
By leaders who make speeches
And take stands
That pander to one group or
another

Few and far between
One rises that speaks truth for all
Holds a candle for a greater good
Who will admit when wrong
And make corrections to the
course

Innocents suffer when that's not
done
Held captive by the whims of
one
Misinformation and falsehoods
Passing the blame for missteps
Accountability a foreign word or
thought

The path ahead is unclear
Shrouded in dark clouds and fog
Where is the light, the guiding
force
Is there a way out
No, it's not mine repeated

July 9, 2020 mkb

24

Two-Edged Sword

Damned if you do
Damned if you don't
A two-edged sword is held
By some who will and some who won't

Hidden alien threatens all
Forcing mass retreat
Unemployment numbers surge
Money tight, little food to eat

Children suffer at these times
Those with greatest needs
No school to fill the gaps in life
While health providers plead

Yet there's a risk of health and death
If alien invades the space
It is stealth and hides for weeks
Right now, it's winning the race

Will time be on the side of home
Will school openings be safe
Playing roulette is not fun
With human lives at stake

Who will craft the better plan
Find the way for all
Is King Solomon around
To answer the nation's call

July 10, 2020 mkb

2020 Vision

Hindsight is clearer or so they say
Instead of looking forward in our days
There is much to learn from looking back
Assessing all of those things we lack

Lessons to learn and new paths to create
All can be helped as we evaluate
What was done right and what was done wrong
What is worth saving as we all move along

Destructive forces are often the key
To push us to look at what we did not see
Sad as it is, 'tis a truth of nature
We look at a crisis as an adventure

Solutions to questions not asked before
Are often found once we explore
Various options and consult with others
To address the needs of sisters and brothers

The world's been impacted by a deadly force
That knows no limits as it follows its course
The young and the old both are at risk
As the virus moves widely at a great brisk

Working together may lead to a fix
A global solution with all in the mix
Except for a country with experts galore
That some in leadership choose to ignore

How will we see this when all is complete
Will there be unity or continued compete
For the way this is handled will mark our days
As how all are viewed in our means and our ways

July 11, 2020 mkb

Rings

Ring around the rosy
Classic children's game
Pocket full of posies
Linked to death and pain

Ring of fire burning
Circle the wagons
Call in the cavalry
Clear out all the cons

Running in circles
Go this way then that
Spiral out of control
Falling into a cosmic vat

Wringing hands, shaking heads
Question and seek
Feel wrung out and done
Drawn and oh so weak

Bring rings of promise
Rings of new hope
Make true commitments
And help all to cope

Draw a ring around it
Shut down the spread
Stop the ongoing circle
Of infection and dead

July 14, 2020 mkb

Winds of Time

Know the data, know the facts
Don't ask, don't tell
No data, no facts
And all will be well

The wind blows through the seasons
At times, a fierce wild storm
Others, a gentle breeze
All accepted as the norm

Blustery forces change the tide
Disparity in full view
Young and old, rich and poor
Always known but now its new

Wants and needs rise to the top
Black, white, brown seem alike
Yet disproportionate
In care and to the spike

Divisiveness reigns supreme
In places far and wide
Unbelievers now converts
Yet science still denied

I'm not seeing what some see
There are truths hiding there
Peeking through the cracks
Ever widening everywhere

All of this ties together
In a world torn apart
Look for answers, move ahead
Can't we just have a restart

July 15, 2020 mkb

Lead the Way

There was a time in this world
Or so I am told
When folks came together
Helpful efforts were the norm
Like Rosie learning to be a welder

Can we harken back to then
Take initiatives
Just like those "good old days"
Find ways to come together
Leading us all to sane and safer ways

Many have stepped up to the plate
Set plans in firm place
In attempts to flatten curves
Keep distances and stay home
Examples for leadership that serves

Businesses must carry on
New ways to be found
Challenges faced far and wide
Creative innovations
For many to have as we find our stride

In these desperate times
Balance is needed
If all did their part, it seems
We could find an end to this
Short term pain for longer term dreams

July 18, 2020 mkb

Legend of a Man

From Selma to DC
Living a life dedicated to freedom
Non-violent preacher and leader
Asking for human decency

Moving forward, moving on
Marching in his youth, speaking with passion
Facing all with dignified determination
Risking life and limb in his homeland

A simple man of great strength
Words of wisdom through the decades
Often not heard by others or understood
Continue on, continue on in service

Join those who make decisions
The conscience of the congress assembled
His legacy and humanity will remain forever
Engraved in the marble of souls and minds

July 19, 2020 mkb about John Lewis

Seek the Best

The masked marauders showed
up on stage
A little too late to be playing this
game
Is it just a ploy due to falling polls
Since science so far has been
largely unclaimed

Restrictions discredited too
often at best
Numbers keep rising, surprises
not there
New lockdowns ensue, debates
raging on
Barn door seems closed, does
anyone care

Those who labor at low paying
jobs
Are trying to live life with little
support
As dollars are given to those at
the top
Is trickle down in any of the
news reports

Truth be told, one country is not
alone
Though now it has climbed up to
the top
Others also seeing resurgence
and spikes
Need global assaults to get it to
stop

Can we start to seek the best for
all
Brilliant minds here and there
put together
Find solutions and preventions
to help
Cap the eruptions one way or
another

July 19, 2020 mkb

How Far Will This Go

Months to go
The race is on
How soon before
We tire of this song

So much at stake
As we face alarms
From near and far
Cities to farms

Two sparring partners
Enter the ring
Start to throw gauntlets
Deliver the stings

Supporters line up
Shouting cheers on the side
Opponents boo loudly
And continue to chide

Positions and statements all in
the news
Truth and lies need to discern
This way and that way
How will everyone learn

When it's all over
Some will be pleased
Others in anger
No way to appease

For now there are weeks
Ahead to endure
The bantering attacks
That leave us unsure

Is this the best way
Can nothing be done
To ease this whole process
When folks choose to run

July 21, 2020 mkb

Looking Ahead

Can't look back
Will only depress
When looking at numbers
And all of the rest

Where we were
And where we are now
There is no compare
Says those with know how

So what's the way forward
To truly progress
And find our way out
Of this global mess

Scholars of science
May find the fix
All in due time
When pieces all click

Until that time happens
All can play parts
Stay away from each other
Embrace in our hearts

Be polite when about
Mask that cough and your talk
Be mindful of distance
When out for a walk

United we have the power to halt
Increases reported far and widespread
So let's be a force
Against all the fear and the dread

A choir has formed
Of those who comply
Now spread the word gently
So others can try

July 21, 2020 mkb

Presence

Mom called us to the table
Come share your gifts with all
Be a presence for others to see
Many answered the call

Come and join the gathering
With those who are in need
To march together and tell their stories
Of strife in the face of greed

Be a support, not subvert
Be calm amidst the noise
Stand strong and free for the world to see
Throughout maintain poise

Prepare to protect self
The truth needs to be told
Forces are working against reason
Time to be brave and bold

Now the words matter most
So raise your voices loud
Presence is the power of the truth
Stay strong, secure your ground

July 25, 2020 mkb

Rollercoaster

Cancelled shows
Cancelled trips
Small prices to pay
Just tiny blips
In the course of the months
Over all the weeks
Unlike many others
As a virus hides and seeks
Numbers keep moving
In directions up and down
A rollercoaster ride of sorts
No screams allowed, only frowns

In all this noise
You've been my calm
Fed my mind
Like a soothing balm
Then a clap of thunder
Off in the distance
Stirs the senses
Forces a sideways glance
Cautions and precautions
Time to double down
Will others follow suit
Before more are gone

July 27, 2020 mkb

Unfamiliar Streets

Where am I these days
These streets aren't familiar
Once walked them with friends
Laughing in long ago years

Trying hard to find grace
But fail with fear and concern
Blasts in everyday news
Will this time lessons be learned

How long before it stops
How far will it all spread
With canisters and batons
And all of the bloodshed

How has it come to this
Who set this path we're on
Decades of history fed hate
Fueled these days by a con

Accusations abound
So many sides point blame
Is there a way to rise above
Will this just all be the same

July 28, 2020 mkb

About Face

Too little too late
Better late than never
Fourth quarter
Time almost up

How will this be played
Who takes the lead
Chess moves in stride
Looking to turn the tide

Uncertainty wages
Bets placed and sealed
Watching in earnest
As players take the field

Sizing them up
Teams are uneven
Supplies misdirected
Intentions though strong

The clock keeps on ticking
Whistles not blown
Play on, play on
As the crowds boo and cheer

It's ancient and new
This game of life played
Like a record on repeat
Same song with new beats

July 29, 2020 mkb

Still Waters Deceive

Rows of cars
Twice a week
Line the road
As food they seek

Needs are great
Resources few
Some step up
Create anew

Kindness of strangers
Communities formed
Neighbors who care
Hope can be restored

His mom once told him
Look for the helpers
Focus on the good
Rather than tempers

We don't always know
The struggles of others
Still waters deceive
The hearts of fathers and mothers

For now, we are certain
There are needs that abound
So, look for the helpers
Where they may be found

July 30, 2020 mkb

Good Trouble

Tell your story
Preach your word
Share your life
Take your stand

Where have you been
That has shaped you
The good, the bad
And the challenges

Reflecting on a life well lived
A courage to step forward
To take a seat at the table
When it wasn't welcomed

Moving forward
Moving onward
Rising to lead
Gentleness personified

Soft spoken words
Peaceful stances
Echoed through the land
Reverberated off the rooftops

So, tell your story
Preach your word
Share your life
Take your stand

Honor the legacy
In humility and grace
Get into good trouble
Go, right those wrongs

July 30, 2020 mkb as we bid farewell to John Lewis

The Statesman

He stood erect
With reverence
And amazing grace
Eloquent words
Care in his eyes
Comforting
Those in grief
Humor interspersed
Spoke truth to power
Reminded the world
A statesman exists

July 30, 2020 mkb

August 2020

Mother Nature joined the fray with wildfires that spread over California and other states in ways that have been termed apocalyptic. In light of the pandemic, school took on a new look with most systems moving to full or partial virtual classes. The two US political parties held their conventions and clearly demonstrated the differences in view about the seriousness of the ongoing pandemic. Internationally, a massive explosion in Beirut initially caused concerns for terrorist activity, but sadly, the damage and loss of life from it was the result of ammonium nitrate that was stored unsafely. John Hume, a key leader in Northern Ireland for peace, died, leaving a legacy of respect and unity. Chadwick Boseman, a young actor who inspired millions with his portrayal of superhero Black Panther, died at the end of the month. Black Lives Matter remained at the forefront of the news, sadly, with the shooting of another black man by police in front of his children. Immigration restraints tightened and thousands of refugees were left stranded on the other side of the US border.

A Bridge Too Far

We'll come to that bridge
When we get to it
A bridge too far
Carrying the weight of the ages
Across the ocean
Across the centuries
Bleeding on the pavement
Rising up in song
Alleluia from the depths
Lamentations, consternations
The holds below
The cabins above
Ancestral ties
Traced through tales
Lost in the stories
Connections skip a generation
Changes the reception
All blend together
In the history of the times

August 2, 2020 mkb

In Memory

Along the row of houses
Behind the walls of life
Assumptions can consume
Lead to decades of strife

Challenge those presumptions made
Respect the differences from our birth
Value dignity and grace within
The collective humanity at its worth

A man dared to look beyond
Dreamed of days with calm and peace
He led a nation in a plan
Where animosities could cease

Seek not that which divides
Look for the commonalities
Embrace the vast uniqueness
Celebrate all the diversities

He is a model for the world
A beacon on a shining hill
Lighting the path for others to take
May his words and actions lead us still

August 4, 2020 mkb in memory of John Hume

A Man Named John

A nation mourns
And celebrates
A life that mattered
And thwarted hates

He came in peace
To calm a land
Words of strength
Carried with a gentle hand

He dared to dream
Calm over storm
From near and far
To mend hearts war torn

The troubles had gone on for years
Fear to walk the streets at times
Visitors would stay away
Caution if one crossed the lines

The land now thrives
Sense of pride restored
Unity in hearts of most
With new hope to look toward

So go forth and live his dream
Light a candle in his name
Carry the legacy of this man
Bear his torch and his flame

August 4, 2020 mkb with thoughts of John Hume and NI

Beirut

It started as a routine day
Going along in a merry way
No one could have known
What would evolve in their home

A small fire at the port
Barely noticed at first look
The white plumes of smoke
Rising up, then all hell broke

A massive explosion shook them all
Broken glass in every hall
Blood and death by the score
Is it an enemy at their door

Human neglect now to blame
Lack of leadership now in shame
Devastation far and wide
So much damage in and outside

The human toll to hearts and minds
Is felt around the world that binds
Us all together on this earth
When we look for all's value and worth

August 6, 2020 mkb

Circle Game

As legislators debate
And continue to disagree
A family goes hungry
More than once a day

Fear increases
Of losing a home
While pundits argue
Don't understand the facts

"Free" money is never free
A price is paid by others, true
All contribute for the good
As economy connects

We spend, you spend
Try to help each other out
Small and big alike
Business is at a slow churn

Jobs are not aplenty
Virus brings a new fear
Working in close quarters
Could be a death knell for all

Close down and stay home
Keeps folks away
Shops and restaurants suffer
Limited buyers, limited income

It is a circle game we play
One hand to another
Who buys, who pays
What is the price for all

August 9, 2020 mkb

Collective of Souls

Protect and serve
Be there for each other
With care and concern
We are sisters and brothers

All put in one place
At a moment in time
A collective of souls
All yours and all mine

Isolated these days
Some far from home
Unable to travel
Too far to roam

How will this be remembered
In books and in lore
As decades pass
And archives are stored

When stories are told
And history reviewed
Down through the years
What will be revealed

Can things be done
Can words be said
That generations from now
Will look back and reflect

Protect and serve
Be there for each other
With care and concern
We're all in this together

August 10, 2020 mkb

Welcome Mats

Let me learn the language you speak
So we may get to know each other well
You have come into this place
In ways that I could not foretell

You traveled far and wide across this land
To reach this far flung port
Arriving with others here
Of same and different sorts

All come for some new adventures
And a better way of life
Hope and dreams a driving force
Away from pain and strife

Welcome mats not always out
In places where you land
May hearts begin to open up
And lend a helping hand

August 11, 2020 mkb

Divisible for All

Churn the waters
Turn the tide
Who's for this
Who's for that
Lift the veil
Unearth the stories
United for
United against
Divisible for all
The wizard is pulling the plugs
Pushing the buttons
Delivering the non-deliverable
Pull back the curtain
Mirrored ball spinning
Scattered lights
Cover the floor
Delusions
Illusions

August 15, 2020 mkb
With thoughts of the USPS

One Nation

I shed a tear
Not for what is
Rather for a dream
One nation truly indivisible
No pledge of allegiance
No national anthem
No thoughts and prayers
Will bring that forth
To be a truth honored
Courage, honesty, respect
For all under one sky
Justice and equality
Equity with unity
To hold diverse views
Share thoughts cordially
Consider all sides
Find a common place
To settle as one nation
Will bring truth in the words
Of a pledge and an anthem

August 17, 2020 mkb

Internet School

No one's waiting at the bus stop
Around the corner of the house
Parents are in the classroom
Set up in rooms here and there
As students zoom in to teachers
Dedicated to deliver their very best

Lessons well planned
In new ways to share
Try to keep interest
With some who don't care

Many will struggle
Others will thrive
Familiar stories
Highlight new drive

May all be safe
Maintain their cool
As screen time increases
In that internet school

August 18, 2020 mkb

It's a Process

Promises made
Promises kept
Promises broken
Promises inept

Come together
Only a dream
Held in a pipe
So it may seem

Hope shines bright
In hearts of many
As plans are made
In the land of plenty

May the best come forth
Healing begin
New horizons arise
Depending on a win

August 18, 2020 mkb

Leadership

How does one follow
How does one lead
In times of want
And times of need

Fires are burning
Earth shakes below
Illness invades
Strong winds blow

Damage, destruction
Many must face
Deal with the loss
Left in the place

True leaders arise
Answer appeals
Rebuild communities
Repair and heal

They come down the street
They come from distant lands
They come together all
Focused one in hand

Servant leaders turn to follow
Grassroot followers take the lead
Serve each other well
When crisis brings a need

August 19, 2020 mkb

Measure of a Person

How does one characterize a person
What frame of reference is used
How does one determine criteria
Where does one look for clues

Words and actions expressed in the light
May not reflect one's true nature
Quiet movements, whispers in the dark
Gifts given in private may be more sure

Seeking accolades and recognition
May get the attention desired
Often will unveil shallowness
Too much ego acquired

Deferring to the grace of others
Allowing shining stars to rise
Support and encouragement
Show the person as a prize

May all find ways in the months ahead
To build foundations of care
Prop those in our lives up
In this world that we do share

August 22, 2020 mkb

Precipice

Teetering on edges
Prepare, withdraw, remain
Stay the course, stay informed
Which way to go to just stay sane

The punches keep coming
How can one deal
Coping skills fading
Not sure how to feel

Times have been odd
So much in our way
Nature and humans
Make it hard to just play

Rise above it we will
Find connections to love
Seek that which pleases
Give more than enough

Reaching out to those present
With a word or a deed
May ease one's concerns
And fill a self-need

August 24, 2020 mkb

Overwhelm

There is an isolation
That creeps into the soul
When forces outside one's self
Begin to take their toll

Such has been the struggle
And indeed the pain
For many in our world
So much loss, little gain

They may not be known
Unheard and unseen
Striving to survive
In times seeming so mean

It's been a year enduring
Almost never-ending
Four months left to go
Perhaps a time for mending

Holding those who suffer
In mind and heart
May healing find its way
And all get a new start

August 24, 2020 mkb

What of the Children

Children witness a parent shot
Reminds me of another
Someone I once knew
Who became a loving mother

Pain in both these cases
Justice served for one
Life now in balance for the other
Not sure yet what will be done

Today's too common of a story
Facts still to unfold
Meanwhile questions remain
For hearts and minds to hold

August 25, 2020 mkb

Looking for Hope

Why even say we'll learn
History repeats and repeats
Centuries, decades, years, months
All pass two steps forward
How many more behind

Looking for hope
Parents plead
Sister is numb
Children ask why
Protests, looting, confusion
More lives pay the price
Misinterpret, misrepresent

Color of skin
Religion
Where one lives
Age, gender, who one loves
All rationale given
Festering hate

History repeats and repeats
Centuries, decades, years, months
All pass two steps forward
How many more behind
Why even say we'll learn

August 26, 2020 mkb

What Have the Children Learned

What have the children learned
Losses of their innocence
In an instant, over time
Two cases in an incidence

Worlds apart yet now connected
In ways hard to fathom
Sadly it is all too real
Making me feel numb

It's said that it takes a generation
For changes to come true
Years from now what is the legacy
From lessons now in view

In the end so much is lost
For all those lives impacted
Judgments made right and left
About some laws enacted

Again, I ask what can be done
To stem the hatred tide
Is it possible to come together
And listen to each side

August 9, 2020 mkb

Talking Points

Late adopters
Lost the war
Claim to win
The battles
The fires rage on
Borders once open
Closed again
Facts bend
Like blooms seeking sun
Talking points
Same response
Different questions
Anyone can put on a show
Measure of character
What is done
When prying eyes not looking

August 30, 2020 mkb

Other Options

What can be done differently
To get the points across
How can platforms be shared
That lead to gain, not loss

Don't stoop to a bully's level
A lesson shared with sons
Through their growing years
Don't incite the other ones

Assembling is a right
Used effectively for years
Now agitators invade the space
Leaving ruin and tears

Are there other options
To state sound claims
That can be heard
Without these deadly games

August 31, 2020 mkb

September 2020

COVID continued to spread in the US but shows some signs of trending down in parts of the country. It had been in decline in other parts of the world and there was greater hope of re-opening more businesses and activities than had been done so far. The events leading to the shooting of Breonna Taylor by police officers in March came more to light. The Presidential debates started and only exacerbated the divisiveness. Unemployment due to the shutdowns with COVID continued to increase, leading to more and more financial concerns. One of the most notable events in this month was the passing of Ruth Bader Ginsburg, Supreme Court Justice, and the rapid replacement for her seat of a philosophically polar opposite judge. This was also in stark contrast to a previous Supreme Court opening in 2016 that was delayed due to it being in an election year. The announcement of the new Justice's nomination was held in a garden gathering that became known as a super-spreader event of the virus.

Out of Context

All is in full throttle
Brief clip here
Short message there
Sixty-one days to go
How many sound bites
Filter, unfilter
Truth and lies
Can't erase
Criticize
Supersize
Exaggerize
Microwave world
No time to digest
Tomes or even paragraphs
News reports little help
Try to get to what's real
Perceptions cloud the way
Just spell the name right
Mode of the day
Sixty-one days to go
And counting

September 3, 2020 mkb

New Steps

Discern
Re-learn
New steps
Once known
Slowly break out
Cocoon enclosed
Brave new world
Changed yet familiar
Following paths well traveled
Months, years before the now
Existence of calm amidst calamity
Move gently in the spaces
Lest the fabric be disturbed
Embrace at a distance
Maintain the peace
Follow the trends
Lead the way
New steps
Re-learn
Discern

September 4, 2020 mb

Winners and Losers

How do we define the win, the loss
Who is in the lead and who falls behind
The hare and the tortoise taught lessons
In the younger years, lost through time
Power, wealth, authority often measure
Success determined by some in those seats
Heroes rise on other platforms
Often in the shadows, in the quiet of the night
No fanfare, no press release, no megaphone
Giving of self, serving those in need
Paying the price of duty with their life
Who truly are the winners and losers
In this game of life as it is played
By those who adhere to standards
Next to those who may not hold tact
How do we define the win, the loss
Who are your winners, your losers

September 6, 2020 mkb

Solomon's Wisdom

Alliteration, illumination, illustration
Repeat once more
Light the way
Paint a picture
So all may see
The path that lies ahead

Confusion is now
This way or that
Much said
Little learned
Wash, rinse, repeat
Nothing new
Same stains

Church and state separate
No more for some
Who is right
What is wrong
Narrow focus
Limited views
Global perspective lost
Amidst all the noise

Who is worthy
Who is not
Who is to decide
And how
Where is Solomon's wisdom
Now

September 7, 2020 mkb

Wind

A gentle breeze greets my day
Cool autumnal air a joy to feel
I revel in the grace of nature
Grateful to be in the state 'tarheel'

Then the news crackles on
Wind brought rain and destruction
To lands not far from here
Friends now deal with devastation

Further reports of windswept flames
Others with belongings packed
Waiting to leave their homes and goods
Should the fires change their tack

Sweet Baby James in my head
With his song of fire and rain
Reality of those not so pleasing
Resulting in loss, sorrow, and pain

I sit with thoughts of friends
Helpless in so many ways
With hope in my heart and mind
For calm to take hold in their days

September 9, 2020 mkb

Purse Strings

Purse strings held by others
Seeming not to care
Or truly understand the dire need
Of those with nothing to spare

Time has passed endlessly
Or so it certainly seems
For many lost to worry and fear
A shattering of their dreams

No help seems on the horizon
If others have their way
Those who could provide the funds
Just seem to run away

The kindness of the locals
Neighbors and town folks
Strive to fill the gaps in place
Since the leaders last spoke

So who truly holds the purse strings
Of those in cities and towns
When neighbors count on others
To help when they are down

September 11, 2020 mkb

Anticipation, Exhilaration, Trepidation

A pin falls on the carpet
A tree falls in the forest
A silent heart yearns
To sing out in joyous refrain

Waiting for an embrace
Waiting for coming together
Waiting for a noise from others
To sing out in joyous refrain

Silence fills the voids
Silence echoes in empty halls
Silence longs for all
To sing out in joyous refrain

September 13, 2020 mkb

Heroes

They come from near and far
Giving all they can
Asking nothing in return
Trying to dampen the fan
That blows the flames
Ravaging the land
Up and down
The coast of hills and sand
Their work is day and night
Sleeping on the ground
Eating when they can
Unknown when homeward bound
More will now be in another place
To answer nature's call
And face the winds that will bring
Damage from a water wall
Too often heroes are unsung
Or elevated to that state
Through sports or entertainment
That somehow doesn't relate
Let's take a moment or two
To truly appreciate
Those who come to our aid
When forces seek to eradicate

September 15, 2020 mkb

Campaign Non-reform

Back to back
And back and forth
Front to back
And back again
The cash register rings out
Singing the tunes across the land

Truths, lies, distortions
Snippets of a word or two
Challenging to listen to
Tune in and tune out
Argue, debate, criticize, rationalize

The money requests
Come fund here or there
It is needed to share the word
Make a case in public court
For this, against that
In a 30 second blurb

It's campaign season in America
A time of rancor and discord
Not unlike other lands it seems
With passion taking over reason
Competitors rising up to strike
Facing all that comes their way

September 16, 2020 mkb

Distractions

Months of same days
Only so much can be done
With minutes and hours ticking by
In isolation for a party of one

Find new avenues
Travel some paths unknown
Explore interests not before tried
All from the comfort of home

Distractions abound
Music and books, courses online
Providing a world of numerous options
Easily found all in due time

Could now sit for hours
Roaming the net around
Never leaving the couch of comfort
While still being homebound

Time to move more I dare say
Before the nearby potted plant
Starts to show more growth than me
And I become irrelevant

September 16, 2020 mkb

Rest in Power

The power of one
Not with might of muscle
Not with force of fist
Not with strength through stature
Rather with words spoken
Rather with thoughts conveyed
Rather with deliberations in earnest

The power of one
To call for justice
To strive for understanding
To raise the bar higher and higher
Through actions of reason
Through decisions against odds
Through advocating for those in need

The power of one
Now gone from our sight
Now lost to the history
Now remembered with praise
Rests in the legacy
Rests in the edicts written
Rests in the hearts of many

September 18, 2020 mkb
Remembering RBG

Courage

Peace and justice
Commonly said
Along with truth
As we are led
Along a path of right and wrong
By those who came before
Trying to show a better way
To hold value at the core
The way is not always straight
As challengers arise
To tempt and lead one astray
With promises of a prize
From time to time we get to see
A thoughtful leader in our midst
Who through their wisdom
Can transcend all the dimless wits
There is time to stop and revere
Those who pass before us
To take the time to honor them
Let many grieve and wait to discuss
Replacements are hard to find
Ones that carry merit
And can ease the pain of loss
Of one who had courage to dare it

September 20, 2020 mkb

Hypocrisy

You say this now
To suit your needs
But those were not
The words or deeds
Shared years ago
In another time
When things were not
For you, all fine
You took a path
Clearly planned
To put off decisions
In spite of demand
It now comes back
With a new twist
A shortened time
But now is your wish
To hastily vote
Upon a court case
That defies your own acts
An amazing about face
It cannot be denied
Or swept away
Others are speaking
And will have their say

September 23, 2020 mkb

Say Her Name

Speak it clearly
Repeat the name
Not only hers
Others are the same

Let it be an anthem
For injustices we see
Ill-defined regulations
Of what is allowed to be

May peaceful voices
Continue to rise
Not be distracted
By those who revise

Speak out the truth
Stay the course
Justice will come
With votes, not force

To honor those gone
Hold their names up high
Champion the cause
Though others may defy

September 23, 2020 mkb

More Words

Words uttered
Words spewed out
Words that seek to divide
Words that carry clout

Words that defy
Words that question
Words that impact
Words that others mention

Words that are false
Words that negate
Words that incite
Words that foster hate

Words spoken freely
Words shared worldwide
Words about ballots
Words meant to chide

September 23, 2020 mkb

Stately Lady

Stately lady
Lying in state
Honor her
On this date
And days going forward
As her memory
Is carried
In hearts and minds
In lace collars worn
In decisions to be made
May others raise their voice
With dignity and grace
For causes great and small
For finding truth
For seeking justice
For finding common links
Stately lady
Lying in state
Honor her
Remember her

September 24, 2020 mkb
RIP RBG

North Star

Core strength
Core values
To the core
In all the news

North star
Guide a path
Hold the course
Face the wrath

True to self
True in deed
Unlike others
Who hold false creed

Going forward
Keep in heart
Truth and honor
Right from the start

September 27, 2020 mkb

Childhood Messages

Pay the piper
Walk the walk
Steady hand on the till
Talk the talk

Imbalance in nature
Chicken Little may have been right
The sky is falling
Or seems like that in the light

Max went a rompin'
Through the night and the day
His monsters in tow
Running and playing during his stay

The path is now rocky
The emperor strolls the streets
Don't understand
Support of those he meets

Some try to speak truth
To tell an honest story
Let's be more like Max
Not the emperor seeking glory

September 28, 2020 mkb

Bully Pulpit

Trying to breathe
Inhale, exhale
Count to seven
Got to three, epic fail

Recover my senses
Try to accept
Challenge to do
Too much lack of respect

Try to make points
Unable to say
In spite of rules
Interruptions mainstay

Where do we go
What can be said
Do we need more
Is democracy dead

This is not right
Not true debate
Can this just end
Or sadly, more our fate

September 29, 2020 mkb

Integrity in Play

The pawn has been moved
Once more played in a game
Positioned to strike
When the queen was lost
How does it feel
To stand as a model of righteousness
Yet be manipulated and used
In such a hypocritical way
Integrity is doing the right thing
When no one is watching
All eyes are on you now
And you play along in this farce
There is no justice here
Merely pieces on a board
One trying to outsmart others
Through the veils of lies
Use my words against me
One player once said
No honor now shown
And the game carries on
Just because one can
Doesn't mean one should

September 30, 2020 mkb

October 2020

The election in the US remained at the forefront with so much discord that the presidential debate required a mute button to be put in place. The pandemic showed signs of ramping up more and more. The US President was hospitalized after testing positive yet still downplayed the illness in part since he received experimental treatment.

Tracing

The ostrich keeps it head in the sand
Refusing to come out and take a look around
No plans, no ways, no awareness in the land
For the invisible cloud that is wayward bound

The turtle stays tight in its shell
Refusing to come out and take a look around
No plans, no ways, no awareness, no one to tell
About the invisible cloud that is wayward bound

The chicken runs around to and fro
Refusing to slow down and take a look around
No plans, no ways, no awareness, no place to go
From the invisible cloud that is wayward bound

The dog barks out its warning
Asking others to come out and take a look around
With plans, and ways, and awareness of mapping
To help track the invisible cloud that is wayward bound

October 2, 2020 mkb

Seven

Reliving a moment in history
A time of tremendous unrest
Still remembered
Now memorialized
In film to tell the story
Beyond the news reels
And the press
Unrest, some common themes
Repeating, repeating
Never ending
So it seems, yet
In between the hatred and the strife
Moments, almost fleeting
Full of grace and joy and care
Not as celebrated or reported
Still they are there
Shining stars in those times
When everything feels right
Beacons ever glowing
To show us love and hope and light

October 5, 2020 mkb

Shooting Arrows from Horseback

Distortions of time and space
Seem to be taking place
Twilight Zone was a tv show
It's now a part of the flow
Words and actions recently shared
Cannot be compared
To anything of reason or sense
Rather they just make many tense
A known agent in the air
Is now widely being shared
Clear targets not in view
Can be scattered over more than a few
Traveling across the land
Accompanied by the band
Taking aim in spite of facts
Like shooting arrows from horseback
Now more are at risk
Tsk, tsk, tsk

October 4, 2020 mkb

Lessons

In the land of non-believers
A lesson was delivered
Harsh as it may be
Was needed to be considered

The stage was set in the garden
A cast of hundreds at the ready
Some had already learned the truth
Others held their views steady

It spread with ease and without care
Young and old alike were touched
One by one they soon found out
Not wise to be unmasked and bunched

Some would think the lesson took
That now a message would be shared
To follow public health restrictions
Rather it appears that so few cared

All those who have succumbed
Are left behind or so it seems
Survivors told not to fear or change a path
As one leading non-believer deems

October 7, 2020 mkb

Seconds Anyone

Here we go yet again
Words are spoken
Ones heard before
No news broken

Did it make a difference
Depends on who you ask
Most minds have decided
So seems a futile task

Who won the match
Much still left unsaid
Undecideds swayed at all
We'll see if any have been led

Final choice will be made
Four weeks yet to go
Tighten belts and hold on fast
There's still much more to know

October 7, 2020 mkb

Cacophony

Early morning calm along the road I stroll
Rhythm of the music keeping a steady beat for my feet
Colors burst from every tree against the dawn's early light
No pretense or lies as nature unveils new sights and scents
Up ahead a cacophony of noise fills the branches and sky
Blackbirds a plenty, all cawing at once, can any be heard
Rising, rising upward and swooping low as if one
Circling above the trees until sufficient branches found
A stillness settles, an eerie quiet, watching, waiting
A lone chirp rings out, a throaty song that echoes and fades
Pause for a moment and question the meaning, the message
Search through the memories of time, reminisce, people and places
All is connected and the rhythm keeps a steady beat for my feet

October 10, 2020 mkb

Truth to Self or Not

Volley back and forth
Ball is in which court
Depends on how you view
Decisions in a tort

Determination done
Guess we'll soon find out
Seems to be such a sham
Abuse of perceived clout

Do as I say not as I do
Seems to be the lesson here
Once taboo to even consider
Now is how they steer

How must it feel I wonder now
To be used in the political game
What are the expectations
In the end can you be the same

October 13, 2020 mkb

What Channel Are You On

To be-lieve
Or not to be-lieve
What channel are you on
Truths, lies, stories
Connecting, distancing, dueling
Many already decided
Mind made up
Vote's been cast
Sit back now and watch or not
Unfolding, updating, unending
Ads, news, analysis, criticism
Nineteen days, keep counting
Keep breathing, keep hope
New intrigue enters last minute
Foreign in its nature
No surprises with that
Déjà vu all over again
To be-lieve
Or not to be-lieve
What channel are you on

October 15, 2020 mkb

Countdown

Let the countdown begin
10, 9, 8 to blast off
Will all engines fire
A smooth soar rise
There's certainly fuel
Being added daily
Balanced, unbalanced
Even out the ballast
Possible, not sure
Unlikely it seems
Reports indicate
Key players strapped in
What will fly
In days ahead and beyond
Stay calm, it will unfold
True characters revealed

October 23, 2020 mkb

As Live as It Gets

Through the glass I reach for you
So near and yet so far
Cliché, it is true
Like the nighttime moon and star
Distance makes the heart grow fonder
So the saying goes
This time apart is killing
No doubt my sadness shows
As we share a moment or two
Across the screens shining
Over the miles and the time
Our new connection defining
This is as live as it gets
During these days apart
Longing for the touch of you
Feeling the pulse of your heart
For now this is the best it can be
So, through the glass
I reach for you
Until our isolation shall pass

October 23, 2020 mkb

Lessons Taught

Malign another's character
A tactic used by many
Every election season
What is the rhyme and reason

Is that truly behavior that we want
Our children to learn is right
Thought we wanted to try to curb
Words that don't border on the absurd

Do as I say not as I do
Can't be the mantra here
Since both words and actions
Point in nasty directions

Those who share their views
Who have a plan in mind
Can enunciate in a clear way
Less likely to cause us all dismay

Hoping the fourth will be with us
A decision firmly made
Discord finally put aside
But sense that hope will be tried

October 24, 2020 mkb

The Cynic Within

Nothing will change
It will all stay the same
The bickering and complaints
New players, new names

Decades have shown
There are them and there's us
Whoever they were or who they are now
Are either believed or not held in trust

Important decisions are made
Some large and some small
How they play out in the world
May not matter to most at all

How to live with all this
Depends on your view
Treat each other with kindness
Is not a message that's new

Prophets and guides
Have given us clues
Over centuries through teachings
To follow if we so choose

The cynic within
Is not sure that will be
Guess time will reveal truth
In my dreams it will be

October 25, 2020 mkb

Last Days

Breathe I keep reminding myself
All will be done in less than a week
That is the master plan at least
Navigating the news and double speak

Looking for truth amid all the polls
Many second guessing each minute
Pundits and pollsters and newscasters all
Everyone declaring they're in it to win it

Global eyes are keenly held captive
Curious in ways I'd never have thought
Felt I was fairly astute of world news
These others show they are very well taught

With so many keeping their fingers now crossed
For a certain outcome of the race
Can this global hope carry us through
And get everyone off this frenetic pace

October 28, 2020 mkb

Dominoes and Masks

Masks here, masks there
Covering mouths and noses
Fancy designs now on the market
To be styling in all our poses

Available online and in every store
Sewing tips and patterns shared
Cottage industries popping up
Used by all of those who have cared

It's an easy way to help stem the tide
Rolling all across the world this year
Rising again in places once thought at ease
New lockdowns now feeding new fear

We are all one on this big blue globe
Dominoes lined up and fall in time
One after another impact them all
And unwanted numbers rise and climb

So what's the lesson to be learned
Masks are everywhere to be had
Put one on and stay at a distance
Be a force for good and not for bad

October 29, 2020 mkb

November 2020

Election day came and went without incidence except in the rhetoric of fraud due to the mail-in ballots expressed by the current President who was not re-elected. Lawsuit after lawsuit ensued in an attempt to overturn the election. All failed. Concerns about the upcoming Thanksgiving holiday becoming super-spreader events were shared with pleas for everyone to stay home. Those pleas were not followed and many traveled by land and air during this time. Days and weeks later, COVID numbers went up as expected. Refugees in Europe faced the cold in camps that also saw fires damaging parts of those camps.

Exhausting

Lockdowns two and three
Taking tolls on you and me
Universal emotions we jointly share
Alone together, we try to care
Fatigued, worn out, exhausted are we
Familiar faces we really don't see
Familiar voices we've not really heard
But loudly written through song and word
Filling space, time, souls, and hearts
A collective bringing all our separate parts
A connection undefined, supporting each and all
As the worldwide force is again at a stall
This now seems unending, not finite
It had been thought a safe path was in sight
Things will never be viewed the same
Forcing us to look ahead, it's a brand new game
So, let's be gentle with ourselves and others
This is exhausting for ours, yours, and theirs

November 1, 2020 mkb

Days to Come

One more day
A favorite song
Has new meaning now
As we face the unknown

One more day
Will all be revealed
How will results be met
Can discord and rancor cease

One more day
Anxiety is at a high
Highways are blocked
Intimidation seems to reign

One more day
Is that really the truth
Not sure how it will go
Many more days to come

November 2, 2020 mkb

Game On

It's game day in America
Not the Super Bowl
World Series
Stanley Cup
Or even NBA play-offs
No, this is the game of politics
The game of democracy at work
Laid out centuries ago
By men (no women) of wisdom
In that day
An experiment in how to lead
How to run a new country
Built upon the best ideas from old ways
Taking out that which did not serve
Seems to have fallen away from ideals
Set as the foundation of governance
It's game day in America
Much hangs in the balance
Let's see how this plays out

November 3, 2020 mkb

On the Fence

Here we sit
The fence is high and strong
No way right now to get down
Waiting for a ladder
On one side or the other
Delivery promised to come
Not assured it will be on time
Not assured it will be right height
Not assured it will be secure
Not assured it will stay

Patience is required
Sitting on our hands
Straddling on the top
Leaning back and forth
Crowds gather on both sides
Cheering and jeering heard
Assured that there is interest
Assured that there is passion
Assured that there is concern
Assured that there is fear

Humpty Dumpty fell down
Not put together again the fate
May that history not repeat
Let's just sit calmly and wait

November 4, 2020 mkb

Where Do We Go From Here

Protracted
Retracted
Distracted
Redacted
Detracted
Reacted
Discounted
Recounted

Lawyered up
Both sides say
Concerns now raised about
Legit votes on election day

System called into question
Democracy on the line
Where do we go from here
Is this only a sign of times

Election reform in the plan
Going forward given all this
What has been learned since decades ago
So we can vote in confident bliss

November 4, 2020 mkb

This Day Forward

The decision is made
Time to come together
Today, some are elated
Not the same for others

Let us find a way
In our communities and towns
To unite in a way not recently known
In all the likely ups and downs

The path may not be easy
To traverse through the coming days
Let's keep the promises made to each other
To support whoever won as best that we may

November 7, 2020 mkb

Moving On

This is how it goes
A change in leaders set
Plans to move ahead
Not accepted by all just yet

Wasn't that long ago
When it went the other way
Acceptance was a challenge
And continues to this day

Shoe is on the other foot
Words used against some in past
Now being practiced by those
Who don't like the die that's cast

Division is an easy out
Pointing fingers there and here
Blaming and shaming is a sad way to be
Perhaps in time unity will appear

Heal the soul of our nation
Were the words shared tonight
During an acceptance speech
May it be so for those left and right

November 7, 2020 mkb

Words Matter

Was reminded by a friend today
About how words have power for us all
In our thoughts and written text
Spoken to others with no recall

How we twist and turn a phrase
Can make or break a conversation
Lead to a new understanding
Or promote misinformation

Can we find some common ground
And start to chat anew
There are things that we all want
Though we may have a different view

Sharing perspectives on a topic
May lead to middle ground
Where decisions can be made
To benefit a lot of folks around

So can we reach out across the aisle
In neighborhoods and towns
Around our country and our world
As we use our verbs and nouns

November 8, 2020 mkb

Measuring Cup

Hold the cup at eye level
When pouring the liquid in
To get an accurate measure
Mom shared as a baking hint

Seems to be a good life lesson
When considering a person's traits
The eyes reveal so much it seems
Showing their loves and their hates

As one shares their thoughts and views
The words they choose are important
How they position themselves can also show
If those words are what they truly meant

Seeing eye to eye may not be possible
As we all move through challenging days
No easy answers and lots of questions
What is the recipe that leads to healing ways

November 9, 2020 mkb

Calm Demeanor

To sit in calm demeanor
In the face of trials and tribulations
To stand with grace and dignity
In the face of worldwide speculations
To rise with compassion and strength
In the face of sheer determination

Challenges and struggles have not been strangers
Faith with love carries one forward
Persevere and carry on
Truth rises to the top, leading to one accord

Time will determine how this will be viewed
Winners and losers all in one place
Coming together may be a dream
Yet always possible after the race

November 13, 2020

Progression, Transgression, Regression

So few steps forward
Giant leaps back
Numbers rise beyond the pale
New records set
Not the number one we want
Calling on better angels
To raise the voice of caution
Decelerate with brakes of reason
While the accelerator goes lame
Bring hope to be believed
Honest evaluation and guide
As the leaves change color
Throughout the fall
From the top down
Through the branches
May progression make changes
To correct the transgressions
That have led to regressions

November 15, 2020 mkb

El Paso in My Heart

Clouds like mighty glaciers rise
Above the horizon and linger
In my mind the golden sky
As dusk settles just past my finger

Pointing to distance while recalling
A time this week a year ago
Visiting a place I had not been
A gift they did kindly bestow

Upon me in my heart with grace
Celebrating and caring those who walked
Across the line on earth through
A river and a bridge clearly marked

Aching for their current pain
Inflicted like many others around
The world right now but more for some
Help and beds are not easily found

All under the same sky above
Trying to find our ways below
Kindness and compassion shared
Can spread love for a long way to go

November 15, 2020 mkb

Ch...Ch...Changes

Changes ever evolving, transforming
Not always the same but yet they are
Challenging for some, taken in stride for others
Making transitions coming close but no cigar

Handling adjustments takes courage
A might and strength of character undefined
Recognized in those who have it and those who don't
Promises made and kept while critiqued and maligned

Moving forward in challenging times
Lessons from the past as guides
Reflect responses of those in the limelight
Sinking in the mire or rising with the tides

There are no easy answers when faced with the new
Striving to carry on as best we can in faith and hope
Through the different paths or ways of being in this world
Perhaps the best way to handle it all is just try to cope

November 17, 2020 mkb

Done…. Not Yet

They answer the call
Bells ringing down the hall
Reverberating and tingling
In their ears never ending
Service and duty drive
A passion as more arrive
Facing an enemy unseen
But known on micro-screens
They ask for adherence
To requests that make sense
Stay safe in your town
As they mask, glove, and gown
Caring for those who keep coming
The song ever strumming
They scream 'oh, I am done' in their minds
Then give even more to all who they find
As they make their rounds
Accept assignments, hit the ground
Running to help stem the curve
Meeting the needs of all who they serve
Applause on doorsteps long ago stopped
As numbers seemed to have dropped
With wave upon wave now rising high
Honor them now and heed their cry

November 21, 2020 mkb

December 2020

Just as pleas went out in November to stay home and not gather to celebrate Thanksgiving, those were echoed about Christmas. Just as they were ignored by thousands in November, the same was true in December. Just as the Thanksgiving holiday impacted the COVID cases, Christmas gatherings did the same. Internationally, more countries returned to stricter lock-downs. The first vaccines became available in the US. At the same time, a variant of the virus was discovered in the UK as well as a number of states in the US. The Supreme Court ruled against lawsuits brought forward to nullify the election results in a number of swing states as part of the ongoing accusations that the current leadership lost due to fraud.

You Can't Make This Stuff Up

Pardon me, you say
Who's at fault
Who's to blame
How these things are thought
Planned, connived, contrived
Beyond reason or sense
Etched in the very fabric
Woven over time
Generations
Passed along as life
Lessons to be shared
For success in the world
Who's at fault
Who's to blame
Pardon, I dare say not

December 1, 2020 mkb

Messaging

Trying to make a point
Limit characters to use
Must be smart and clear
Give a reader perfect cues

If explanations are needed
Will rethink the phrase
Words to be shared
To clear up any haze

Rallying cries must be clear
To gather needed support
Twists of words confuse
Can lead to message distort

Recent slogans for justice
Taken out of context
Argued back and forth
Will see what comes next

Can understanding be gained
With even more words written
Messages tweaked and changed
Finding new ways for them to fit in

How about some dialogue
Discuss what needs be said
Face to face and heart to heart
Maybe try that instead

December 2, 2020 mkb

Ho-Ho-Ho

It's now the holiday season
Time for goodwill and cheer
Sharing it all a bit different
As 2020 is not a usual year

Striving to stay safe
In the face of a vicious virus
Leads to creative endeavors
In celebrating for every one of us

From retailers to deliveries
Ingenious ways to satisfy wishes
New products on the market
To address the current issues

Still with all that is ensuing
The ho-ho-ho bottom line reason
Remains the same with joy and peace
As the messages for the season

December 5, 2020 mkb

National Upside Down

You don't like how it ended
Short end of the stick
Pout and argue it all unfair
Don't understand how you tick

The voices of the masses heard
Choices all were made
Another came out ahead
Time for you to fade

Instead upside down and turned around
Agents try to change it all
In your name and your support
Undermining democracy's call

Political theater such an old show
The curtain coming down
More important issues face us now
As illness is all around

Time to move this show along
The numbers have come in
Wish for your gracious departure
Not likely with the other's win

December 10, 2020 mkb

Ongoing with Hope

Hope we place in decisions made
Rolling out the cure
Rolling up our sleeves
Ready to stop the virus for sure

Celebrations across the land
Healthcare workers at the fore
Happy to take the shot
Promote vaccines for evermore

Cautioned to stay the course
As new lockdowns now in other lands
Keep the distance and mask up
Isolate and remember, wash those hands

December 15, 2020 mkb

Last Page of the Book

I turn the pages one by one
Captivated by the words
The story unfolds in unique ways
Meandering down the hall
Climbing up the stairs
Through the forest
Over the nearest hill
Cascading down the waterfall
Crossing the ocean wide
Music plays unlike before
New characters arrive
Bringing creative gifts
Sharing words of wisdom
Marking notes in margins
Through days and weeks
Months into a year
Life unfolded in 2020
In a different sort of way
Ready to finish this one now
At this last page of the book
A new one to start afresh
Carrying the story forward
I'll turn the pages one by one
Captivated by the words

December 22, 2020 mkb

January 2021

The new year started with ever increasing rhetoric of a stolen election in the US that culminated in an insurrection on the day that the US joint legislative bodies met to certify the electoral college votes. Five individuals lost their lives due to this riot in which the capitol building was overrun. This was conducted by those who support the current president and who were encouraged to take action by him. Legislators who objected to the votes from a couple of states are now being asked to resign. On January 13, articles of impeachment were passed in the Congress after the vice-president chose not to enact the 25th Amendment.

On January 20, President Biden and Vice President Harris were sworn in amid a greatly scaled-down ceremony and armed guards. Meanwhile, a variant of the coronavirus was discovered globally as numbers continued to soar that resulted in more lockdowns and travel restrictions.

Keep Telling Myself

All will be well
No need for concern
Ruminating in my head
Over and over
The story is told
Fact or fiction
Hard to discern
Trust no one
Trust everyone
Trust oneself
Truth in justice
Where is justice
On doorsteps and in hallways
Echoes of liberty
Freedom but not for all
Pundits and pawns
Bullies on pulpits
Undermine
Underscore
Underserve
All will be well
No need for concern
That's what I keep telling myself

January 4, 2021 mkb

Turning Tables

Much on the table
Turning slowly
Same song being played
Over and over and over
Scratches in the vinyl
Remixes in the works
Waiting for new releases
Artists arriving on the scene
Twists to the tunes
Protest songs to be replaced
With hope and reason
Not yet determined
Time will tell what plays
Time will tell who dances
Time will tell how it sounds
Turning tables in our world
What is on your playlist

January 5, 2021 mkb

A Moment in Time

Looking in the mirror of a nation
Reflections of insurrection
Born out of lies, fear, despair
Not in the name of integrity
Not in the name of righteousness
Not in the name of justice
In a world of divisiveness
Unprecedented
Unseen
Unknown
Through decades
History will tell the tale
A day remembered like others
That define a moment in time
Days forward will determine direction
May the phoenix rise from the ashes of a fallen democracy

January 6, 2021 mkb

Knead the Dough

I knead the dough
Listening to the spoken words
Shared by the tv newscaster
Recounting events in my land
Showing the strength and fragility
In the experiment of democracy
A young nation by world standards

I knead the dough
Pondering events in my land
Senator election changes
While other instigates chaos
Disruption in anger leads to death
Destruction in the heart of the capitol
Furnishings can all be replaced

I knead the dough
Wondering what is to come
Waiting for the next shoe to drop
Lies continue to fill the air
Trying now to shut down the voices
After so many years of inciting hate
Hearts take time to come together

January 8, 2021 mkb

My Dad's Party

My Dad's party has ended
Guests started to leave long ago
Others lingered in rapt discussion
Seeking ways to stem the blow

Slowly but surely the truth is clear
Need to gather now is known
A new party plan to be arranged
Try to find a congenial tone

Unite with others for solutions
It might take an act of congress
Ironic some might say these days
But worth a try, a full court press

What rises in the future years
Will be interesting to see
A banquet at a table of plenty
Or someone crying it's just for me

January 12, 2021 mkb

Same Tune, Different Song

Déjà vu
All over again
Same tune
Different song
Playing out
Throughout the land
Come together
In new united ways
Dreaming of a change
To be, who knows
Marking days
Waiting for news
See how it plays out
Take up the case
Yes or no
Agree, disagree
How will they choose
Lines in the sand blur
As stories unfold
Hearts and heads engage
History now being told

January 13, 2021 mkb

Etched on Our Souls

You could still hear the music
Long after they've gone
Story after story
Etched on our souls
Memories of those
Cared for through weeks
Echoes through time
Sounds of life once led
Ring down the halls
Fill the silence unspoken
Songs they well loved
Books they have read
Family and friends dear
Now not allowed near
Holding their hands
Moments of touch
Sharing with loved ones
A visual link
As they fade from this world
Last words to speak
The tears we shed inward
Til exhausted, collapse
You could still hear the music
Long after they've gone
The few notes informing
A life has moved on

January 16, 2020 mkb

Melting Pot

Melting pot
Term often used
Meaning not always shown
Thrown around
Try to explain
Coming together how
Variety is the spice
Walk in different shoes
Modeled for us today
One family
A mosaic
A snapshot
A representation
Immigration gifts
Melding and blending
Steps together
Faiths embracing
One nation
One world
One gathering
Melting pot

January 20, 2021 mkb

Perspectives

Different views
Each unique
A horse
Rivers
Snowcapped hills
One painting
Perspectives
Images vary
Turned this way or that

Different views
Each unique
Honest
Falsehood
Facts, fiction
One newscast
Perspectives
Words vary
Turned this way or that

January 22, 2021 mkb

Looking for Light

'Darkness comes like clockwork every day'
As the song once heard does say
It envelops all around in blackness
Out my window as the light is less and less
In my mind the curtain is closing
Ongoing isolation enfolding
The tunnel is longer
Despair is ever stronger
Looking for light as I peer in and out
Searching for answers here and about
Hands reaching across the divide
Encouraging to take things in stride
A touch, a smile, a connection
The timing and words with perfection
'Darkness comes like clockwork every day'
As that song heard does say
'But then the daylight follows too'
The words do help with the care from you
Reaching out to others during these times
Can make a difference for all our minds

January 25, 2021 mkb
Lyrics by Gary Lightbody from The Curve of Earth by Snow Patrol
and the Saturday Songwriters ©2020

February 2021 – Postscript

As a final nod, for now, to everything in the past year, the second impeachment of the former US President took place.

History in the Making

And so it begins
The case and debate
Playing out for the world
The history books to be
Opening statements done
No surprises there
More to come in the days ahead
Let's see who is prepared
Who is able to make their point
Will any change their mind
Predetermined before today
Will facts sway one way or that
Stay tuned, we shall see
Tomorrow is another day

February 9, 2021 mkb

Moments in Time

Culpable, accountable
What do these words mean
How are they being lived
By those with a political lean

Who is swayed by polls
More than justice and morals
Pictures shown, words expressed
Pain still felt throughout the halls

Do your job as best you can
Deal with trauma in public eye
Relive a moment over and over
There is reason for all to cry

Moments in time captured
For all the world to see
History books will analyze
As for now, this is how it will be

February 10, 2021 mkb

Those Who Serve

Preserve
Protect
Not just words
Spoken
Written
Lived by some
Interpreted
Twisted
Losing meaning
Respect
Defend
Those who serve
Ignored
Trampled
In frenzy of hate

February 11, 2021 mkb

Allegiance

To whom do you owe your support
Who holds your soul in their hands
How do you make your decisions
For those who live in these lands

Words have been spoken for and against
You chose to accept some but not all
History will now determine so much
In time we'll see how it will fall

Consequences to be determined
Days, months, years, decades ahead
The political game playing out
Future party line now possibly dead

Power lies in those who step up
Go forward and decide to run
Take the action to cast a vote
In time we'll see who truly won

February 13, 2021 mkb

Index of Titles

Index by Topic

Elections and Legislative matters

Inspiring Leaders

- North Star (Ruth Bader Ginsburg vs Rep Senators) - 80
- Rest in Power (Ruth Bader Ginsburg) - 74
- Stately Lady (Ruth Bader Ginsburg) - 79
- The Statesman (Barack Obama) - 40

International and Refugees
- A Bridge Too Far - 42
- Beirut - 45
- Distant Voices - 2
- El Paso in My Heart - 113
- Welcome Mats - 48

MK Brennan is a published researcher and author, volunteer editor of textbooks and journal articles, and past Chairperson of the Writing Committee for the Massage Therapy Foundation. She is co-editor of an anthology, *Patchwork Poetry and Other Gibberish by The Saturday Songwriters,* that features over 100 poems, prose, and works of art by 39 individuals from over a dozen countries. Her professional experience includes working as a nurse, massage therapist, health promoter, and in research methodology. Additionally, she has held various leadership positions in non-profit associations and organizations. All of these experiences help inform her writings. On the personal side, MK has three adult sons, two daughters-in-law, two granddaughters, and one grandson. Two mixed breed dogs keep her company and active with our daily walks.

Printed in Great Britain
by Amazon